BREAKING THE
GOLDEN POD

BREAKING THE
GOLDEN POD

JOHN MENSAH

authorHOUSE®

AuthorHouse™ UK Ltd.
1663 Liberty Drive
Bloomington, IN 47403 USA
www.authorhouse.co.uk
Phone: 0800.197.4150

Published by AuthorHouse   11/20/2013

ISBN: 978-1-4918-8510-9 (sc)
ISBN: 978-1-4918-8509-3 (e)

*Any people depicted in stock imagery provided by Thinkstock
are models, and such images are being used for illustrative
purposes only.*
Certain stock imagery © Thinkstock.

This book is printed on acid-free paper.

*Because of the dynamic nature of the Internet, any web
addresses or links contained in this book may have changed
since publication and may no longer be valid. The views
expressed in this work are solely those of the author and do
not necessarily reflect the views of the publisher, and the
publisher hereby disclaims any responsibility for them.*

TABLE OF CONTENTS

DEDICATION

This book is specially dedicated to my dear mother for her unconditional love towards her children, as well as other people's children, for instilling discipline, good moral values, modesty and tenacity of purpose in us, and for her continuous support and prayers, which have moulded us into who we are now.

I dedicate it also to a very best friend, Dr Peter Alakija, for his diverse support towards my efforts in attaining my life goals. Peter has been one of the towers of strength in my life, for which I am immensely grateful.

I also dedicate it to Sankofa, which is a charity that I founded in 2010 to help young Africans to make informed choices in life. This book is dedicated to every person, man or woman, young or old, who dreams of becoming successful in life.

FOREWORD
BY LARA RUFUS,
CEO OF CROWNE CONSULTANCY

There is a plethora of support available to charities and voluntary organisations. However, finding the funds necessary to achieve the goals of these organisations can often be the thing that proves to be the most difficult. It can be quite gruelling to have to navigate your way through the proverbial "grant maze", especially if you do not know where to start. Fundraising is an art that requires a skill set. Education is integral to developing the art of fundraising, a fact that many people fail to realise. Trust fundraising can be an absolute minefield to the novice fundraiser.

Public sector cuts mean the fundraiser's task is more important and urgent than ever. Fundraising these days evolves in the contest of frequently changing socioeconomic trends, and this in turn affects the way in which charities raise funds. Fundraising techniques have also evolved in response to these changes. Charities in the United Kingdom have a combined annual income of £11 billion, generated by around 31,000 paid and countless volunteer fundraisers.

The key to acquiring grants, whether from local government or from trusts and foundations, is communication. One needs to be able to plan for the future, communicate one's cause, and explore potential opportunities for working in partnerships. One must also resolve to be a step ahead of the game by learning new techniques to meet these challenges. As a qualified and experienced fundraiser, I know how painful fundraising can be for new fundraisers and small organisations. I know first-hand the struggle they go through to raise funds to survive. I have seen the time and energy wasted in writing applications which get nowhere.

This book provides the reader with a real insight into the ABCs of fundraising, with particular emphasis on fundraising from trusts. It is a fundraising "satnav" and a useful tool to any would-be, and indeed experienced, fundraisers. This book helps identify a starting point and helps readers to navigate their way to their desired destination.

Breaking the Golden Pod is a "must have" book for those beginning their fundraising journey, and it should be on everyone's bookshelf. The explanation of fundraising terms along with step-by-step guides and the list of useful websites is invaluable. It is written in an easy-to-read style, and the simple steps, once applied, are positive contributors towards winning those much-needed funds for your charitable cause. The objective of this book is to be an invaluable companion basic guide to trust fundraising for fundraisers.

I for one will be recommending this guide to others. The pocket form it takes means you can carry it anywhere for an easy read.

INTRODUCTION

The information in this book is based on my personal experiences as a fundraising consultant, my training materials and articles, and the shared views and contributions of friends, clients, and professional colleagues. Some of the information here is also based on secondary desktop research, which involves the summary, collation, and synthesis of existing research rather than primary research. I have made reasonable efforts in checking the accuracy of information used, but I cannot guarantee or take responsibility for any errors or omissions in such information. This book is not aimed at providing academic discourse. It is a simple step-by-step guide for small community organisations and for fundraisers and voluntary sector workers who want to improve their fundraising skills.

1

WHAT IS FUNDRAISING?

Fundraising is about selling an idea or a good cause to someone who has the financial means to make it happen. To be successful at fundraising, you have to be able to convince people to develop interest in your idea and donate their money or time to sponsor it. There are many definitions of fundraising, but for the purposes of clarity, I would like to rely on a few definitions from a variety of sources.

- *Fundraising is the process of soliciting and gathering voluntary contributions such as money or other resources, by requesting donations from individuals, businesses, charitable foundations, or governmental agencies. Although fundraising typically refers to efforts to gather money for non-profit organizations, it is sometimes used to refer to the identification and solicitation of investors or other sources of capital for for-profit enterprises. Fundraising is a significant way that non-profit organizations may obtain money for their operations. These operations can involve a very broad array of concerns such as religious*

> *or philanthropic activities such as research, public broadcasting, political campaigns and environmental issues.* (Wikipedia, the free encyclopaedia)
> * *Fundraising is defined as the collection of money through donations, sales, and/or event programming for the purposes of a charitable donation. (Syracuse University Student Centre)*
> * *Fundraising is the process of soliciting and gathering money by requesting donations from individuals, businesses, charitable foundations, or governmental agencies. It is the primarily way that non-profit_organisations obtain money for their operations. (Wikipedia)*
> * *Not-for-profit organisations depend on fundraising to address specific causes such as raising awareness of issues as poverty, environment, health, gender and children's issues, as well as to provide direct relief direct services to people. (Milos Pesic)*

Fundraising is an act of identifying, recruiting, and developing the human, material, and financial resources necessary for an organisation to attain its goals. It is about achieving the need which an organisation is set up to meet. It is a process of "selling" that need effectively to those who are likely to support it. Fundraising can also be understood as an attempt to pull together the capabilities and resources of individuals and communities. For most organisations, fundraising is often the only way that enables them to gain the necessary funds to attain their goals. It is also considered as an opportunity whereby resources are transferred from those who are able to give to those who have the need.

Fundraising is not about being desperate or begging or harassing people to donate towards your cause. It should not be confused with chasing money everywhere, because too often organisations get confused about the point of fundraising. Applying for a grant simply because the funds are available and not because it will promote your mission is called "fund-chasing". Fundraising is a mutual relationship through which people give money to the work they are passionate about. Fundraisers have no need to beg, as begging is necessary only when you have nothing tangible to offer for what you are asking for. If the organisation has a good cause, then it has the right to ask for money to promote the cause. Fundraising requires the ability to convince people and to sell your cause effectively. Fundraising is an act of gentle and evidence-based persuasion, which takes time, patience, and adequate planning to achieve.

Why Is Fundraising Important?

Charities are set up not to make profit but to raise enough funds to cover the cost of their philanthropic work. Every organisation needs money to survive. The truth is that without fundraising, charities will not be able to survive and their pressing desire to address needs will remain unachieved. Apart from money, fundraising can also help generate other forms of support, such as volunteers, material and in-kind donations, and sponsorships. It can also help an organisation establish a positive profile and enable it to give people hope through their work. Fundraising can create an opportunity for the organisation to connect with wealthy and important individuals and

3

organisations that will give, and also to facilitate successful contacts. There is no doubt about why fundraising is important in promoting an organisation's programmes. As hard and frustrating as raising funds can be, it is important not to forget the significant impact it can make on the organisation and it constituents. In most cases, it is the lifeline of the

Why You Should Make a Good Case

It is necessary to use the best approach to increase your opportunity to mobilise resources. A good fundraising approach would answer the following questions:

> **"If you are doing a good work, then it is important to raise the money to do it.""**

- *What is the need?*
- *Who will benefit when the need is met?*
- *Is the need an urgent one?*
- *Is your organisation qualified to address this need, taking into consideration the fact that there are many other organisations that are addressing or could address those needs?*
- *What is unique about your organisation?*
- *Does your organisation have a good track record?*
- *What will be the benefits of your action? What are the positive consequences?*
- *What will be the negative consequences if your project should fail?*

One thing that is always important to remember is your case statement. This is because it constitutes the basis for your fundraising and development strategy. A case statement clearly states the organisation's mission and vision. It helps tell your donors why you want them to support you, and what outcomes you are hoping to achieve with their donation. Give them good reasons why they should donate to you. Remember that people want to give their money to an organisation that has a compelling case.

The Economic Environment

The voluntary sector is faced with the huge challenge of surviving through difficult economic recessions, reforms, and budgetary adjustments. A tumultuous economy can present unique challenges for charities and can significantly reduce returns on fundraising. Changing socioeconomic trends have made life difficult for these organisations. Smaller organisations are left with no choice but to try and become professional, competitive, and innovative. Governments around the world are re-focusing their economies with new adjustment policies. With increasing austerity measures across the

"A mission statement defines what an organization is, why it exists, and its reason for being. At a minimum, your mission statement should define who your primary customers are, identify the products and services you produce, and describe the geographical location in which you operate." Daniel Morgan

5

board, reductions in income from the public sector, as well as the increased need for services, is undoubtedly squeezing many charities to either shrink their services or close down. Their incomes have fallen while demand for their services is rising.

In the United Kingdom, the government's desire to reduce budget deficits and cut waste in the economy has resulted in major cuts in grants to statutory and voluntary sector organisations. This has resulted in some community organisations closing their services. Cuts are impacting negatively on their ability to deliver. Funders are also cutting back or tightening their criteria in order to ensure that the limited funds available are given to select organisations with strong and compelling cases, thus making it impossible for small organisations to obtain grants.

There are countless small organisations with incomes of less than £10,000 whose work directly benefits hard-to-reach targets, and they are finding it hard to cope with the changes. For such organisations, cuts mean looking for alternative sources of funds to meet the needs of their beneficiaries. Another factor that impacts negatively on their ability to raise funds is the increasing number of charities emerging every year in England and Wales, who are all chasing the same funding streams, thereby making it extremely difficult to access grants.

Lack of professionalism, the absence of the requisite skills in fundraising, stiff competition, and limited human and material resources have all negatively affected small organisations. It is imperative that these organisations begin to look at ways of improving their ability to stay afloat by adopting new business approaches, regularly revising their strategies, and clearly establishing their financial needs, which are all key to improving their efficiencies and indeed to ensuring their survival.

It is true that tough economic changes have caused grant givers to cut back on grants to charities and community groups, and some of you will be saying, "What's the point in applying?" But do not be discouraged or put off your search for grants in tough economic times. Be optimistic and start from somewhere.

Applying for grants is just like investing in treasury bonds. Just keep trying and it will pay off. The solution is not to give up during tough times. It is about reviewing your strategies, and putting in the hard thinking and extra hard work that will help you beat the challenges.

2

WHAT IS A GRANT?

A grant is a sum of money given by a funder to an organisation to enable a project to get off the ground. Grants are not personal benefits, gifts, or loans to organisations or individuals. They are sums of money awarded to finance a particular project or activity for the public benefit. Grants can be given to companies with charitable objects, to charities, and to volunteer and faith-based organisations by grant-makers, such as trusts and foundations, educational institutions, or businesses. Grants can be obtained in two ways by writing a proposal or by completing an application form supplied by the grant-giver. Grants are obtained either on the applicant's own initiative or in response to a request from the grant-giver. For many organisations, a grant serves as the organisation's bedrock or as a means for reaching their goals. Grants are very popular and are beginning to overtake other sources of fundraising such as events, corporate sponsorships, and sales. Grant-giving is a big industry with huge income, yet only a small percentage of applications are funded.

Sourcing of grants has almost replaced traditional fundraising. The majority of charities now prefers grants, to the other types of fundraising. Grant-making trusts and foundations have their own requirements, which have to be strictly adhered to. They are clear on what they want their money to achieve and on its overall impact on the community. Trusts and foundations do not work on the ground or deliver services directly to the communities. Instead they give grants to charitable organisations who work directly with the people. To be successful in obtaining a grant is to demonstrate how your project will help the grant-givers achieve their aim.

Who Gives Grants?

In the United Kingdom, grants are given by a variety of businesses, government departments, trusts and foundations, and local governments, and there are also grants from the National Lottery and international sources. Some wealthy individuals set up foundations while they are alive, or rather than bequeathing all of their wealth to their family, they choose to set up posthumous foundations that will give away money to support causes of their choice. Most corporate bodies also give grants as part of their corporate social responsibility. Grant-givers have their own set of criteria and are more concerned about achievable outcomes and greater impact on the community.

There are some 10,000 independent charitable trusts and foundations in the United Kingdom, distributing about £2 billion in grants annually to community organisations of different sizes. Their giving pattern varies; some give grants locally, nationally, or internationally, while others only give funds to local projects. Grant-givers are charities themselves, controlled by a board of trustees, with paid staff and volunteer panels. Most of them belong to umbrella bodies such as the ASSOCIATION OF CHARITABLE FOUNDATIONS which is a common platform to promote good practices among trusts and foundations and to educate the public about their work. The amount they give is about ten per cent of all income received by voluntary organisations annually. While many charitable trusts and foundations derive their income from endowments, stocks and shares, and landed properties, some grant-givers, such as BBC Children in Need and Comic Relief, raise money from national and public appeals to distribute to good causes.

Types of Grants

The types of grant an organisation can apply for depend on various factors, including their mission, objectives, annual income, legal status, management structures, accounts, and track record. The amount of the grant amount they are looking for and its purpose are also factors. There are different types of grants an organisation can apply for.

- A *kick-starting grant* is used to get a project off the ground.
- A *revenue grant* covers running costs, including salaries.
- A *capital grant* pays for building costs or equipment.
- A *project grant* pays for a mixture of items within a project budget, sometimes including a contribution to overheads and management time.

A few trusts provide a kind of partnership grant known as a *core grant* over a number of years.

Trusts of all sizes often have a *small grants* programme which involves less paperwork and a faster response time.

Grant-givers always fund areas that government does not provide money for. They support issues such as tackling humanitarian problems, vulnerable and disadvantaged children, women and disabled persons, ethnic minority organisations, health, education, social welfare, and poverty alleviation.

Finding the Right Grant-Giver

There are almost 9,000 grant-giving trusts and foundations in the United Kingdom and thousands internationally. Because there are so many of them out there, it may seem a daunting task to try to find those that will be willing to fund your project. Small organisations require a lot of patience, skill, and detailed research to identify the most suitable grant-givers for their organisation. This will help them make an informed decision about the right grant-giver to approach for help. They need to know about the grant-giver, because different grant-givers have different areas of interest.

Use a variety of methods to choose the funder that is likely to fund your project. Make sure you search through various grant directories published by funding agencies and through various online resources to locate them. Approaching the wrong grant-giver with a request for funds will be a waste of your organisation's time and resources, as well as theirs.

Look for grant-givers who support projects within your geographical area. Avoid approaching a grant-giver that does not fund projects in your area. You may consider those who fund projects nationally, but remember that the competition can undoubtedly be stiff. To break through the competition requires hard work and putting forward the right facts to make your application stand out among others.

Look for grant-givers who make grants of the size you require for your projects. Avoid asking a small grant-giver for more money than they give out. This information can be found on their website or in the guidance documents.

Recycling Applications

Much as it is important to collect sample successful grant proposals to use as models or a standard template for future grant applications, it is not advisable to use the same application that has been successful in the past or one that has been used by another organisation without customising it to your organisation's current specific needs. Making the assumption that because it was successful before, it can be used again in its entirety for a different funder is not the best thing to do. This is one of the common mistakes that will lead to rejection by grant-givers. There are multiple reasons, why you should not do this.

Grant applications require much detailed information specific to your organisation and activities and how they fit into a grant-giver's criteria. Using a recycled application may not accurately capture the dynamic of your organisation or exactly what is required by a specific grant-giver. You will be missing or misrepresenting your organisation's priorities. Use recycled or previously successful application only as a guide, because a good application is one that truly reflects your mission and goals.

3

THE FACTORS IN SUCCESSFUL GRANT APPLICATIONS

Leadership

The success of every organisation, whether small or large, depends on good and effective leadership, which can best be described as a process of influencing and aiding others in the accomplishment of a common task. Effective leadership and strategic thinking are key ingredients in successful fundraising. This is why the fundraising sector, under the auspices of the Institute of Fundraising and other allied agencies, is investing in leadership development to create a pool of people with the relevant skills and information to boost income mobilisation within the sector.

It is important for a charity to identify and develop team leaders who will be responsible for leading the process of developing good grant applications and proposals. Apart from leading, this person must commit to being a source of inspiration to others on the team, to communicating with them as a means of motivating and bringing out the best in them, and to knowing what their goals are to determine their level of involvement in the whole process. The leader must take the lead in developing ideas and turning them into practice, lead and manage all activities, including delegating key roles and responsibilities, and above all be enthusiastic about the people he or she is leading

Ideas

Changing socioeconomic trends require strategic thinking and innovation by charities. Think fast and be innovative in order to facilitate the organisation's fundraising objectives. The challenges facing charities are enormous and call for critical thinking, to enable charities to remain engaged with donors and grant-givers. Generating new ideas is necessary, because grant-givers value innovation and originality.

> "If your actions inspire others to dream more, learn more, do more and become more, you are a leader."
> **John Quincy Adams**

Create a database of fresh ideas, but also continue to review what has been done in the past and think of how to make these approaches more innovative in the future. Creativity in all aspects of fundraising is great, but it's only effective if you know how to apply it to the benefit of the organisation. It does require you to think outside of the box to enable you to stand out from the crowd. Be creative in your quest to keep your organisation going, because creativity can maximise your organisation's fundraising results.

4

VITAL STEPS TOWARDS MAKING A GRANT APPLICATION

Before you start making a grant application, it is absolutely important to make sure that you know the priorities of the grant-giver and that your application meets those criteria. Grant administrators often get irritated by sifting through

> **"There's a way to do it better. Find it."**
>
> **Thomas Edison**

piles of irrelevant applications that do not meet stated criteria, while badly prepared applications end up in the bin.

Writing a funding application needs a sober, thorough, and strategic mind in order to persuade the grant-giver that the project merits support. Make sure you are well prepared by familiarising yourself with their criteria before you start.

Get organised and remain focused throughout the period of writing the application. Keep a notebook handy to write down ideas and any relevant information. Review the notes and try to connect with those ideas. Remember not to throw away the notes during the application-writing stage. The notes should be easily accessible. You should also remember to assemble all important documents, accounts or financial projections, governing documents, letters of support, and policies before you commence the application.

Research

The first thing an organisation should do is to research prospective grant-givers before beginning the application. Make sure that you read their guidelines carefully to ensure that you understand what they support. Carry out detailed research to ascertain their criteria and what is required

> "A successful grant proposal is one that is well-prepared, thoughtfully planned, and concisely packaged."
> CFDA

before applying. This will undoubtedly increase your chances of success.

You first have to know the types of projects the grant-giver has funded in the past, the geographical area and the size of grants awarded. Some grant-givers regularly change their criteria, so it is advisable to keep abreast of these changes. If it looks like a grant-giver does not fund a type of cause, it is not advisable to plead for special treatment, as this is highly unlikely to be granted.

Research about a grant-giver can be conducted either on their website, by a telephone conversation, or by requesting the information pack, which will contain all the information on how to apply. As part of your research, you should try to answer the following questions.

- What need is the grant-giver interested in?
- What type of projects are they willing to support?
- Are there any restrictions on how much they will give?

> **"Research is formalized curiosity. It is poking and prying with a purpose."**
> (Zora Neale Hurston)

- Which geographical area does the grant-giver focus on?
- What is the average size of grant and their time cycles?
- Who were the grant-giver's previous grant recipients
- What are the trustees' backgrounds and influences?
- Are there any particular ways of working that the grant-giver is keen to support?
- What types of grant will the grant-giver consider?
- Are there any restrictions on what they will fund?

If you still have doubt or are not clear about any of their criteria, ask the grant-giver to clarify. It is a waste of your time to write to a grant-giver if they do not fund the type of project you are intending to undertake or if what they fund is completely different from what you are asking. Grant-givers have their criteria for specific reasons, and if you fail to meet them, your application will be binned. Therefore, detailed research is one of the means to success.

Consultation

Consultation is very crucial in fundraising, especially when applying for a grant. Consulting other people and the wider community is a sure way to success, because this will help you identify appropriate needs and how to address those needs. It will provide the opportunity for others to join hands with you in developing a winning application and be part of the implementation of the project, which will ensure that the project achieves its desired impact. Community support and collaboration are critical in obtaining grants.

Consultations will afford you the opportunity to identify appropriate stakeholders who will give you letters of support. Letters of support can be persuasive to a grant-giver. Remember that these letters can only be obtained through consultations. They can provide the necessary endorsement and exact levels of commitment to your project.

Identify your stakeholders and why you need each of them, because your quest for grants will be successful with wider participation. Consultation will prove a worthy investment for your organisation. It is also an assurance to the grant-giver that you are not alone. Create a list of key stakeholders, which should include your trustees, staff, volunteers, the local authority, and partners for each project. Once your list is complete, contact them directly to discuss your intended project and their expected input.

Several weeks may be required for these consultations through a series of meetings.

Careful planning for engagement with relevant stakeholders will not only enhance your chances of getting the grant, but it will also provide extra hands to assist in the implementation of the project. It will make you visible in the community and give others a chance to contribute to your work. Remember that fundraising is not the job of only the paid fundraiser, chief executive, or hired employee. It is everyone's responsibility, so get everybody involved in the drive.

Grant-givers often want to support groups that collaborate with others and pool of resources to support your project. Applications from stand-alone groups with no partners and without a viable plan for sustainability beyond the grant period rarely succeed

Planning

Planning is an important process for determining a future course of action. Why take an action? How to take an action? When to take action? Planning bridges the gap from where you are to where you want to go. It is a process through which an organisation achieves its goals and makes things occur. Planning is definitely the pathway to successful fundraising.

Effective planning helps lay out the specific strategies of the organisation. It helps develop a clear picture of your resources and projects and the organisation's short, medium, and long-term goals. It helps determine what grant sources best suit your organisation's needs and when and how to source them. It is also an opportunity to regularly monitor and evaluate the progress of your activities.

Planning the structure of a grant application is extremely important, because a successful *application* is dependent upon a careful preparation. You would be surprised by how many applications are rejected by funders because of poor planning. Research conducted by the Directory of Social Change in 2009 shows that many applications are ineligible and find their way into the bins. This is because of a variety of problems, including lack of coordinated planning for writing structured applications. As a result, many applications made to funders fail. Rejected applications are not only painful but are also a waste of resource for the organisation applying.

Set priorities by making a list of all the steps involved in writing your grant application.

Another important way to write a good application is by sharing responsibility and tasks with staff and colleagues.

- Allocate a person to lead the process.
- Have an achievable deadline.
- Have patience while writing your applications.
- Meticulous planning will allow you to know if you fit into the funder's eligibility criteria.
- Allocate time to conduct your research on a suitable grant-giver.
- Set dates and times to make phone calls to grant administrators.

- Speak to other charities that have been successful in obtaining grants from your chosen grant-giver.
- Set meeting dates and times with relevant stakeholders to discuss the proposed project with them.
- Assemble all your letters of support or written agreements in time.
- Set indicators for feedback, monitoring, and evaluating the process of writing your application.
- Do not leave things for the last minute, as this may affect your ability to meet the grant-giver's deadline.

Gantt Charts

To make your task of writing the application easier, it is advisable to create a chart to give you an overview of the tasks and schedule of writing the application. This will also help you keep track of the work done so far and what is left to do, as well as what resources you would require and who is responsible for doing what.

Example of a Gantt Chart

Task Schedule to plot the task, the people responsible for implementing the task, and the timeline

Activity	Week 1	Week 2	Week 3	Resources	Responsibility
Planning Meeting					
Consultations					
Writing Application					
Submission					
Follow-ups					
"By failing to prepare, you are preparing to fail." (Benjamin Franklin)					

Building Relationships

All fundraising is about relationships, whether it is event, church, online, major donor, or trust fundraising. Relationships are vital for all types of donors. Developing relationships with grant-givers is key to getting grants. As in every sphere of life, relationships can increase your chances of success. Cultivating relationships with potential grant-givers has clear benefits for the success of your application. It pays to begin a relationship with a new potential donor to explain your need and ask for investment.

It can be extremely helpful to establish initial contacts with grant-givers to make them aware of your organisation before submitting your application. However, this may not always be possible with some grant-givers, because they do not have the capacity to deal with enquiries from all potential applicants. The other ways to build a relationship with funders are via telephone calls and through networking events. You may also use your contacts to reach a grant-giver.

Map your networks and use your trustees, staff, volunteers, friends, and past donors to create new relationships with grant-givers. Find out about who knows a decision-making person in a trust or foundation, and ask them to make introductions about your organisation. Asking for funds is the final step in building relationships. Remember that fundraising is about cultivating relationships.

The key to success with grant-givers is good relationship-building. The more personal contact you can get with them, the better. However, you need to be careful and take a balanced approach to avoid becoming a pest.

Communicate relationships professionally and in an honest and transparent manner.

Listen to what they tell you, share information and ideas with them, and they will tell you if it fits into their criteria. Developing a successful relationship with a grant-giver is not a one-off activity; it is a long-term relationship regardless of whether they awarded you grant or not. Endear yourself by being a good steward, because a good relationship needs to be nurtured.

5

WHY GRANT APPLICATIONS FAIL

According to various studies and research many applications made to grant-givers fail to meet the basic eligibility criteria and are rejected for that reason. These applications are a waste of the applicant's time, since they rarely if ever result in grants. They are also a waste of funders' time. Applications fail because of inadequate research, because they present quantity rather than quality of approach, or because they lack a clearly defined need and have missing information.

It is important that applicants know some of the common questions funders ask when assessing an application. Knowing these questions will help you to develop your application within that context.

How do you know this project or service is *needed*?

- Does the project fit into grant *guidelines*?
- Is the organisation *eligible* to receive a grant?
- What *need* is the project aimed at solving?
- Who are the *beneficiaries*?
- How many people will the project *benefit*?

- What is the likely problem the project is trying to address?
- Is the project *achievable*?
- What are the *outcomes*?
- Is the organisation *capable* of carrying out the project?
- Is the organisation *accountable* based on its history?
- Is the *budget* detailed?

The majority of applications fail for the following reasons.

- Applicants do not read the guidelines.
- Applicants do not state clear justification for the project.
- There is lack of evidence of what is needed and the appropriate solution.
- The application does not include supporting information and documents as requested by grant-giver.
- All of correct contact details and the appropriate person's signature are omitted.
- The application is not complete.
- The application is submitted late.
- References are not included requested.
- The applicant did not ask other people to read through and review the application before it was submitted.
- The applicant completes the wrong application form.
- The application is for projects that are not funded.

Some grant-givers will look at your website to see if you do what you claim to be doing in your application. If the website is out of date or seems to have a different emphasis from other descriptions of your organisation, the application is unlikely to succeed. Update your website regularly.

One other reason why grant-givers refuse a grant is when the organisation does not comply with the Charity Commission's reporting requirement. They check to see if annual returns are submitted on time, as failing to do this surely count against your organisation.

Your organisation may lack a significant track record to be considered credible by a grant-giver, especially if you have not shown any initiative to partner with other groups that could increase your credibility.

Starting a project before you apply for grant will not succeed. Grant-givers do not fund projects that have taken place already or are midway through.

Regular training and developing the skills of your trustees, staff, and volunteers is important, because this provides grant-givers the assurance that your team have the relevant skills to manage funds properly.

6

PARTS OF THE APPLICATION

Statement of Need

This is an important area of your application. In it you describe the need you want to address. Prove that you have a significant need or problem by providing relevant statistics or any other research data available. Explain how the wider community will benefit from the solution. Be clear and factual about what the need is and how it was identified.

Project Description

This is where you will explain the purpose of the project for which you are asking for money. This section will include information on how the project will be implemented and what it will achieve. Clearly state your timeline and logistics, including staff and volunteers. Remember to include the following:

- **Goals**—the results of the change that the project is aimed at achieving,
- **Objectives**—specific, tangible, measurable, and time-framed outcomes,
- **Milestones**—short-term achievements that will ensure that your project is on track,
- **Administration**—the people who will be involved in the project and their assigned responsibilities, and
- **Partners**—the list of external partners and brief information about them and their role in the project.

Describe in detail the project and what you hope to accomplish in order to convince the grant-giver that your project is important. Describe the problem and your proposed solution. Focus on how the project will benefit the beneficiaries. Give the grant-giver all the information they want. Be mindful of realistic revenue projections.

Provide honest forecasts, not those based assumptions. Keep it real, as unsubstantiated claims can undermine a good application and create cynicism.

Back your claims with the results of surveys and studies about the problem you are aiming to solve, and do not be afraid to talk about the potential risks or challenges involved with the project.

Replacing the hype with realism and honesty might be a refreshing change for the grant-giver. Your application has to be coherent and easy to understand.

The application should have a clear structure that follows the outline: project title, introduction and summary, the need and beneficiaries, outputs, outcome, how it will be implemented, monitoring of results, and how much money you will raise from other grant sources.

Your project description is an opportunity to provide sufficient information for someone completely new to your organisation and the issues you want to address. Supply the summary of the key components of your application, including project objectives, what's new, and different and critical activities related to the success of the project.

Outputs

State clearly how things will be done in order to achieve the objectives of your project. This will convince the grant-giver that you are organised and will do things meticulously. Outputs are the activities; they describe how you will implement your project. Outputs can include the services or activities you will offer to facilitate what you will do. Your outputs should relate to the objectives of the project.

Expected Outcomes

State clear outcomes that will make real changes to the need you are trying to identify. Be specific about broad goals, measurable objectives, and quantified outcomes. Ensure that outcomes are aligned to the grant-giver's criteria. Tell them exactly what results your project will achieve.

31

It can be difficulty sometimes to develop smart outcomes, especially for organisations whose work is not practical and tangible. This is why you should make sure your project is really needed and will address a particular problem and that it is in line with your mission statement.

Another way of developing smart outcomes is through meetings with volunteers, key stakeholders, and beneficiaries. Ask yourself consistently what you want to achieve from this project. This will help to align the outcomes with those of those of the grant-giver. There is no luck involved in obtaining a grant. It is a very competitive and professional endeavour that requires great care, objectivity, and professionalism. See the samples of good and bad outcome descriptions below.

Bad examples:

"The project will reduce domestic violence against women."

"This project will ensure that homeless young people are housed."

These outcomes are not specific and convincing enough.

Good examples:

"At the end of three weeks of training, twenty-one of the twenty-five youth participants will be able to prepare good CV's that will help them gain employment."

"At the end of the two weeks of training on advocacy, the participants will understand the importance of lobbying."

The best way to evaluate whether the objectives of the project have been met, are to develop a format of your outcomes that should include: **Who** (audience), **What** (action), **When** (time) and **Why** (reason)

Budget

A budget, simply put, is a list of projected revenues and expenses for your project. It is a spending plan that includes everything you will spend money on. Research has shown that some small organisations do not budget for their programmes. This has the tendency to affect the long-term growth of your organisation. Budgeting for a proposed project for which you are seeking a grant has to be done well and with great care. A well-written budget shows the grant-giver that a grant from them would be carefully utilised for the project.

Your budget must make financial sense and must be accurate and mathematically correct. It will tell how the *grant* will be used in the application. Your budget should reflect the project's objectives. Show the grant-giver exactly what their money will be spent on.

A good budget is a big plus for the grant-seeker. Getting it right is vital. It is worth paying attention to preparing a budget that will encourage the grant-giver to give you the grant. A good budget is one that is very detailed and that captures all expenses. Double-check your figures carefully, and include headings such as "Budget Category", "Requested Amount", "Local and in-kind contributions". List all your costs, including:

33

- Personnel (If the project requires that you cover staff costs, you will include that salary under the category "Personnel". If you are hiring new staff, determining the actual salary can be tricky.)
- Volunteer costs
- Travel Costs
- Equipment
- Supplies
- Monitoring and evaluation
- Administration
- In-kind contributions
- Matching costs (If any)
- Indirect costs for grants such as insurance, utilities, and garbage service
- Use the Budget Narrative section to explain any unusual items in the budget.
- Get the calculations right by looking for actual prices for each listed item. Do not guess.
- Assemble all your invoices and evidence.
- In-kind contributions are goods or services that are donated to the organisation. These services and contributions can often be used as "match" by many grant sources. Examples of in-kind contributions are as follows: A restaurant donating food for a community event, An individual donating their used clothes and other items to the charity, In-kind donation could also be donating your time or professional services. This could include regular volunteers or company staff helping with their at events, an expert such as an accountant doing free book keeping for a charity, or a celebrity lobbying on behalf of the charity.

Get your team to help with the budget, because a good budget is the result of co-ordinated input and effort. Remember that grant-givers are interested in detailed and accurate figures.

Sample Project Budget

Description	Cost		Remarks
	Actual	Amount Requested	
Project Planning Activities			
Venue			
Food and Refreshment			
Training Materials			
Facilitator's Fees			
Marketing & Publicity			
Stationery & Printing			
Staff			
Volunteers Cost			
Equipment Hire			
Transportation			
Monitoring & Evaluation			
Total			
Narratives and Comments			

Monitoring and Evaluation

Demonstrate clearly how the project will be monitored and evaluated. These are important tools for determining that results will be achieved. They will also ensure that funds are used effectively, and they will also help you know about the short- and long-term progress of the project.

What you aim to achieve with the provided money has to be captured in your monitoring and evaluation section. State specific Indicators and means of verification, such as data collection, quarterly reports, and focus group meetings.

Unfortunately, many people believe that monitoring and evaluation is performed to keep donors happy, because they require it. Although it is important for donors to know whether their money is being spent properly, the most important reason for monitoring and evaluating is to help the organisation itself to identify its strengths and weaknesses and build upon them. It would also allow you to learn and make a significant difference in the lives of your constituents.

Demonstrate that you will involve users, internal and external people, in monitoring. A well-written evaluation provides the grant-giver with assurance of accountability. Evaluation should concentrate on the way the project was conducted in terms of its usefulness and consistency. Your evaluation must be tied to data collection as part of project activities. The following is an example of the use of indicators.

How the Project Will Be Monitored and Evaluated

Keeping records of all activities related to the project. Records will include the six equalities strands: gender, age, ethnicity, faith, disability, and sexual orientation used for monitoring purposes only.

Collating feedback from beneficiaries through questionnaires, surveys, and observation by our volunteers.

Maintaining an attendance register of participants for each component of the project, including monthly and quarterly reviews of outputs against the projects agreed targets.

Detailed end of project evaluation, incorporating monitoring information, responses and feedback from participants, staff and volunteers, statistics and other data coming from the project.

Long-Term Sustainability

In simple terms, sustainability means the ability or capacity to endure. Long-term maintenance is a responsibility that has economic and social consequences and that demonstrates the concept of stewardship. Every organisation has to think of the long-term sustainability and maintenance of its programmes. Lenders, banks, grant-givers, and corporate sponsors all require a programme to demonstrate sustainability as a means of achieving long-term goals.

Grant-givers would not like to fund a project for a short time. Before they invest in the project, they will want to know your organisation's plans for sustaining the project into the future, after their help.

Provide specific information on how the organisation intends to raise the required funds to continue operating the project. Focus attention on the sustainability of the project by thinking of how to carry it forward after the grant funds are finished.

Demonstrate to the grant-giver the long-term financial viability of the project. Tell them how you will continue the project without relying upon them for permanent commitment. Here are some examples.

How to Sustain the Project after the Grant

The project will be sustained after this grant is finished through the following:

- We will obtain grants from other funders to enable us to continue with future follow-up projects.
- We will work closely with stakeholders, including local businesses, who will be asked to support the future of the project.
- We will rely on increased income from continuous fundraising programmes to sustain the project.
- We will establish a social enterprise to engage in charitable trading and plough profits back into our charitable activities, including this project.
- We will charge beneficiaries fees for the services provided.
- We will use the Internet and social media to provide easy means for donors to give online.

Review

From the outset, identify a team who will provide support in writing your application. Let your team help you review the application in order to help fill in all gaps and spot possible errors.

- Keep your application brief and simple. A simple and readable application is likely to be successful. You may be used to writing in a particular style that is easy for your team or members to understand, but remember that grant-givers are not part of your organisation. They also do not have the time to research the details of what you have written.
- Keep it real. Provide the grant-giver with facts and figures, not long essays.
- Focus on the positive. Do not provide grim statistics and stories of suffering, because grant-givers do not want to be part of failure.
- Do not sound desperate or beg grant-givers for money. Ask them to be a partner in a good project.
- Stay within limits; do not exceed required numbers of words and the like.
- Edit the application. It is important not to rush in writing your application. Give yourself a minimum of two weeks to do a good job. Leave about five days to edit.
- Ensure that your sentences are short and succinct, and avoid repetition.
- Avoid shrinking the font size. This makes the application difficult to read.
- Use simple and plain language, avoiding jargon, big words, and acronyms,
- Make your application neat, well labelled, and error-free.

7

SUBMITTING YOUR APPLICATION

Make it a point to submit your application to the grant-giver early. Mail it ten days prior to their deadline, and use the remaining time to lobby your request through phone calls. If the application is to be posted, make sure you attach a good cover letter that states the title and a brief description of the project. Do not wait until the last minute. If the application is to be emailed, do not hit the submit button until you are sure that is ready to be judged. Keep a copy of the application and all the attachments for reference in case the grant-giver asks for further information.

Appendices

Common attachments include:

- Research, surveys, and survey data
- Governing document
- Résumés of key personnel
- Annual reports and accounts
- Policies

- Brochures, photographs, leaflets, and press cuttings
- Letters of support
- Cover letters
- Referees
- Do not include attachments unless they are vital to the project or have been requested by the grant-giver.

8

FOLLOW-UP

After you have submitted your application, give the grant-giver a quick call a week later to check whether it has been received and whether any further information would be required. Send them any additional information requested on time. Celebrate if the application is successful. Remember to acknowledge receipt of the grant and promise to keep the grant-giver informed on the progress of the project.

Reporting

Your relationship with the grant-giver does not end with the receipt of the grant. Some grant-givers request periodic reporting, whilst some may ask for it at the end of the project. Some also request site visits to evaluate the progress of your project. Sending the grant-giver a good report has multiple benefits, including the ability to ask for support again. It also reflects the organisation's honesty and responsiveness.

Submit your project reports on time. Show that you have utilised the grant well and made good progress. This is an opportunity to go back to the grant-giver and ask for more funds. If you are having problems submitting report on time as specified by the conditions of the grant, quickly inform them of the problem and assure them that it will be submitted as soon as it is sorted.

It is worth noting that submission of your accounts and annual returns to the Charities Commission and Companies House is very important, because grant-givers will not give you a grant if you default in this area. It is a risk that they are not prepared to take. Failure to lodge figures with the Charity Commission is the most common reason for rejection of grant bids.

> "Thank you" is the best prayer that anyone could say. I say that one a lot. Thank you expresses extreme gratitude, humility, understanding."
> (Alice Walker)

Accountability

Transparency is crucial to the well-being of an organisation. Charities and fundraisers must show accountability for any income raised and how those funds are used. To this end, a system for handling accounting should be developed and should run efficiently. Not only must all the finances be clearly accounted for, but fundraisers will find information regarding the amount of money raised via different activities helpful. Donors will also request receipts and will want to know how their money is spent. Being able to provide them with this information enhances the credibility of the organisation, makes the donor happy, and helps to build a strong long-lasting relationship.

Rejection

The hardest thing for every fundraiser is when their application for a grant is declined. Grant-givers have limited resources which are to be used to achieve maximum benefit, and that is the reason why some requests are rejected. If your application is rejected by a grant-giver despite all your hard work, do not be depressed and don't let it get to you personally. Take it as a learning process towards future success.

You should muster the courage to call a grant-giver and find out what was wrong with your application and how it could be improved in future. Ask them when you can resubmit another application. Stay in touch and inform them of your organisation's progress.

Thank Your Donor

Taking care of your donor by saying thank you is an appropriate way to show your appreciation. Most organisations do not say or send thank-you notes to grant-givers, because grant-givers are perceived to be faceless.

> "We learn wisdom from failure much more than success. We often discover what we will do, by finding out what we will not do."
> (Samuel Smiles)

Remember that trusts and foundations have people working for them just like any other organisation. They would appreciate the fact that you recognise their support. Let them know how much their gift is appreciated and what it will help your organisation achieve.

9

HELPFUL TIPS

Switch on and get informed.

Make sure you find out what support is available to your organisation and how to access it.

Keep updating your organisational information.

Have a realistic fundraising plan. Some community organisations, especially smaller ones, do not have a fundraising plan. Their fundraising activities are based on ad hoc arrangements. This is definitely the wrong way to run your organisation. Fundraising without a plan or strategy is a recipe for stress, headaches, and failure.

It is necessary to have a well-written fundraising plan, no matter the size of your organisation. A good fundraising plan will let you focus your efforts and plan out your yearly fundraising goals and tactics to achieve them.

Work as a team. Much is achieved through collective effort.

Assess your strengths so that you can concentrate on doing the right things at all times.

Network! It helps you develop new relationships and helps you understand the people who are important to your work.

Create a database of funders and donors.

Be honest. There are basic principles to bear in mind when fundraising, but by far the most important is honesty. No matter who you are or what you are fundraising for, you need to be as upfront and honest with donors as possible. The more transparent the sector is, the more trust and confidence the public will have in the sector. It is vital that funds raised from the public or from grants is used as intended by donors. If you raise money for a specific purpose, you have to use the money for this purpose.

It is often helpful to include a secondary purpose when asking for money to allow more flexibility in spending the money. For example, if you are raising money to buy equipment you could say that any money that cannot be spent on that piece of equipment will be donated to charity, or used for X purposes. This can be particularly useful if you raise too much or too little money or if circumstances change. (Source: Institute of Fundraising)

The Institute of Fundraising has created the "Accountability and Transparency Guidance", also known as "The Code of Fundraising Practice". It provides guidance on how to interact with potential donors and the type of information that should be shared.

If an organisation finds itself raising multiple funds or money because they contacted several funders about the same project, it is extremely important to be honest by informing all of them about the situation and asking for alternative use of their funds, such as expanding your project or increasing the number of beneficiaries.

- Always keep donors informed.
- Use materials over and over again.
- Never apply to one funder.
- Credibility is the pathway to success. People want to support worthy and trusted organisations.
- Demonstrate success and keep track of your progress.
- Be strategic, not reactive.
- Update, inform, and stay engaged with your donors, beneficiaries, and community.
- Tell a story. Everyone likes to hear good and successful stories.
- Do thorough research, because many bids end up in the bins due to poor research.
- Develop some Unique Selling Point (USP) that makes your organisation stand out from others.
- Be specific. Nobody appreciate vagueness or open-ended statements. Provide facts and figures.

Be bold. In every facet of life, boldness is required to enable you to reach extraordinary heights. The same applies in the charity sector, especially in fundraising. It needs passion and boldness to reach our financial goals in order for the organisation to promote its cause. Fundraising is about *passion* and *boldness*. You can do it by simply being bold and taking on the challenge.

Beat the competition. Successful fundraising is a great source of joy, but competition for the sources of funding is fierce. No matter how good your cause, if you submit weak grant applications or deliver fundraising on ad hoc basis, you are going to lose out. It is essential that you make your bid for money stand out from the crowd.

CONCLUSION

Writing a grant application is time-consuming and takes a lot of energy and concentration. It can be both difficult and fulfilling, but simply following the guidelines set out in this book will greatly increase your chances of success. Remember once again that a good application will require diligent effort by carrying out detailed research, collecting information and filling in all appropriate details. Overall, there is no right or wrong way to complete an application form or write a proposal, but you have to bear in mind the that the grant market is very tight and competitive, so you have to get your act right in order to enable your request to stand out among others.

This book has provided you the basic steps necessary to get you started with your winning grant application. The best piece of advice is to follow it through, and you should be successful.

APPENDIX 1

SOURCES OF SUPPORT

If you do require any support after reading the book, here are some suggested organisations you may contact.

Outreach Management Services

Outreach Management Services is an award-winning charity consultancy that specialises in providing cost-effective services to voluntary sector organisations such as charities, faith organisations, and social enterprises, as well as individuals. Outreach provides strategy, organisational development, training, fundraising, project management, and mentoring support to third-sector organisations. In addition to its unique services, which are based on extensive knowledge of the needs of the voluntary sector, it also have a deep understanding of the needs of black and minority ethnic organisations and communities.

Outreach offers services that promote successful implementation of projects and programmes, and it is able to work with organisations on a variety of initiatives ranging from short- to long-term basis. Outreach inspires clients to turn their vision into reality through sustained working relationships.

The author of this book is the founder and CEO of Outreach Management Services. Visit our website for more information. www.outreachmanagement.org.uk

Black Fundraisers UK

The Black Fundraisers UK is a special-interest organisation of the Institute of Fundraising, working to support fundraisers from the black and minority ethnic communities by providing regular forums to meet, share experiences, and access professional support. This unique organisation creates a platform for black professional fundraisers with a common vision and fundraising experience. info@bfuk.org.uk.

Institute of Fundraising

The Institute of Fundraising is the professional membership body for United Kingdom fundraising. It's mission is to support fundraisers, through leadership, representation, standards-setting and education, and we champion and promote fundraising as a career choice. www.institute-of-fundraising.org.uk

Professionals

Do not be discouraged if you don't have the right person in your organisation to write grant applications for you, or if using professional grant writers is too expensive. Look internally for someone you could train to write applications. He or she might be a volunteer or board member.

If you do feel that you need a professional, don't hire one because you think it will be an instant magic solution. Be careful of the professional who promises that his work will yield one hundred per cent success. Look for the one who will tell you the hard facts and who is also willing to work with you on educating and transitioning your organisation to do it on your own. Don't let your preconceptions keep you from reaching your goals.

APPENDIX 2

FAVOURITE QUOTES

"In this business, life is one long fund-raising effort." **(Alvin Ailey)**

"I have found that among its other benefits, giving liberates the soul of the giver**." (Maya Angelou)**

"Giving money effectively is almost as hard as earning it in the first place**." (Bill Gates)**

"Fundraising requires both optimism and realism. Without the first, few if any gift solicitation efforts would be made. Without the second, few if any would succeed**." (Howard L. Jones)**

"We make a living by what we get, but we make a life by what we give**." (Winston Churchill)**

"Generosity consists not the sum given, but the manner in which it is bestowed**." (Mahatma Gandhi)**

"Be the change you want to see in the world**." (Mahatma Gandhi)**

"Joy increases as you give it, and diminishes as you try to keep it yourself. In giving it, you will accumulate a deposit of joy greater than you ever believed possible." **(Norman Vincent Peale)**

"Charity sees the need, not the cause." **(German Proverb)**

"Good actions give strength to ourselves and inspire good actions in others." **(Plato)**

"The way you get meaning into your life is to devote yourself to loving others, devote yourself to your community around you, and devote yourself to creating something that gives you purpose and meaning." **(Mitch Albom)**

"As one person I cannot change the world, but I can change the world of one person." **(Paul Shane Spear)**

"Happiness is not something ready-made. It comes from your own actions." **(Dalai Lama)**

APPENDIX 3

USEFUL WEBSITES FOR RESOURCES AND FUNDERS

Institute of Fundraising www.institute-of-fundraising. org.uk	www.wellcome.ac.uk William A Cadbury Charitable Trust	Rufford Foundation www.rufford.org
Charity Commission www.charitycommission. gov.uk	Wates Foundation www.watesfoundation.org.uk	Ragdoll Foundation www.ragdollfoundation. org.uk
Charity Trustee Networks www.trusteenet.org.uk	Thames Community Foundation www. thamescommunityfoundation. org.uk	The Prince's Trust www.princes-trust.org.uk
Directory of Social change www.dsc.org.uk.	Charities Information Bureau www.cibfunding.org.uk	Trustfunding.org.uk www.trustfunding.org.uk
Fundraising Standards Board www.frsb.org.uk	The Sutton Trust www.suttontrust.com	Northern Rock Foundation www.nr-foundation.org.uk
HM Revenue and Customs http://www.hmrc.gov.uk/	Scottish Community Foundation www. scottishcommunityfoundation. com	Ove Arup Foundation www.arup.com/ foundation
National Association for Volunteer and Community Action http://www.navca.org.uk/	SHINE (Support and Help in Education) www.shinetrust.org.uk	Paul Hamlyn Foundation www.phf.org.uk
NCVO http://www.ncvo-vol.org.uk/	The Pilgrim Trust www.thepilgrimtrust.org.uk	Northern Ireland Voluntary Trust www.nivt.org
The ADAPT Trust www.adapttrust.co.uk	Jack Petchey Foundation www.jackpetcheyfoundation. org.uk	Nationwide Foundation www. nationwidefoundation. org.uk

Church Urban Fund www.cuf.org.uk	Lloyds TSB Foundation www.lloydstsbfoundations. org.uk	Kleinwort Benson Charitable Trust www.drkw.com/ aboutdrkw/community
www.cumbriafoundation.org Clore Duffield Foundation www.cloreduffield.org.uk	Greater Bristol Foundation www.gbf.org.uk	Goldsmith's Company's Charities www.thegoldsmiths.co.uk
County Durham Foundation www. countydurhamfoundation. org.uk	Frieda Scott Charitable Trust www.friedascott.org.uk	Francis C Scott Charitable Trust www.fcsct.org.uk
Esmèe Fairbairn Foundation www.esmeefairbairn.org.uk	FunderFinder.org.uk www.funderfinder.org.uk	Big lottery funding distributors: • www.nesta.org.uk • www.uksport.gov.uk • www.biglotteryfund. org.uk • www.hlf.org.uk • www.awardsforall.org.uk • www. olympiclotterydistributor. org.uk ww.biglotteryfund. org.uk/prog_myplace.htm
Association of Charitable Foundations— http://www.acf.org.uk/	Grantnet—www.grantnet.com	Funding Central— www.fundingcentral. org.uk
City Bridge Trust—www. bridgehousegrants.org.uk	Tudor Trust—www.tudortrust. org.uk	City Parochial Foundation—www. cityparochial.org.uk
Comic Relief www.comicrelief.com	The Henry Smith Charity— www.henrysmithcharity.org.uk	Big Lottery Fund—www. biglotteryfund.org.uk
BBC Children in Need— www.bbc.co.uk/pudsey		
This is not an exhaustive list of funders in the UK. It is just a snap shot of the many funders.		

.

www.ingramcontent.com/pod-product-compliance
Lightning Source LLC
Chambersburg PA
CBHW030519290526
45786CB00004B/1538